Deep Roots

HOW TREES SUSTAIN OUR PLANET

NIKKI TATE

ORCA BOOK PUBLISHERS

Library and Archives Canada Cataloguing in Publication

Tate, Nikki, 1962-, author
Deep roots : how trees sustain our planet / Nikki Tate.
(Orca footprints)

Includes bibliographical references and index.
Issued in print and electronic formats.
ISBN 978-1-4598-0582-8 (bound).—ISBN 978-1-4598-0583-5 (pdf).—
ISBN 978-1-4598-0584-2 (epub)

1. Trees—Juvenile literature. 2. Trees—Ecology—Juvenile literature. I. Title. II. Series: Orca footprints

QK475.8.T38 2016   j582.16   c2015-904476-6
                 c2015-904477-4

First published in the United States, 2016
Library of Congress Control Number: 2015944487

Summary: In this work of nonfiction, the role of trees in maintaining a vibrant ecosystem, as well as providing food, fuel and shelter, is depicted through photographs, personal stories and facts.

Orca Book Publishers is dedicated to preserving the environment and has printed this book on Forest Stewardship Council® certified paper.

Orca Book Publishers gratefully acknowledges the support for its publishing programs provided by the following agencies: the Government of Canada through the Canada Book Fund and the Canada Council for the Arts, and the Province of British Columbia through the BC Arts Council and the Book Publishing Tax Credit.

Cover images by Mahlia Amatina/mahliaamatina.com, and Hero Images/gettyimages.com
Back cover images (top left to right): Claudiad/istock.com, Sugiyono83/dreamstime.com, Isabel Poulin/dreamstime.com (bottom left to right): Hafizismail/dreamstime.com, Max Earey / dreamstime.com, jcamilobernal/dreamstime.com

Design and production by Teresa Bubela and Jenn Playford

ORCA BOOK PUBLISHERS
www.orcabook.com

Printed and bound in Canada.

19 18 17 16 • 4 3 2 1

Trees are useful in many ways, but perhaps best of all they are beautiful to look at and good company on a sunny day.
NADEZDA KOROBKOVA/DREAMSTIME.COM

For Dad and all the trees we planted together.

Contents

CHAPTER ONE: EARTH

CHAPTER TWO: AIR

CHAPTER THREE:
WATER

CHAPTER FOUR:
FIRE

Introduction

When the flowering plum tree outside my window bursts into blossom, it's a sure sign spring has arrived. The tree also reminds me that the world is always changing. Good or bad, nothing lasts forever. ANA VODUSEK

No matter where you live, even if it's in a big city, chances are you won't be far from a tree or two. It's a good thing we find trees all over the place. Not only are they beautiful to look at, but they also provide shelter and food for all sorts of plants, insects and animals. We humans find them pretty useful too. Sometimes called the lungs of the planet, trees are critical for producing oxygen, cleansing both air and runoff water and feeding the soil. We build with their wood, burn them for fuel and enjoy the tasty fruit and nuts some produce.

I think about trees every day. My writing desk faces a big window, which looks out onto a flowering plum tree. In the winter, the tree's bare limbs are black against gray, rainy skies. If we get a big snowfall, I hustle outside to shake the branches to try and prevent them from snapping off under the weight of the snow. As the weather starts to warm in the spring, I watch for the first signs of buds. Before I know it, the tree is festooned with brilliant pink blossoms. During the warm days of summer, birds flit in and out of the leafy branches, and I sometimes take my cup of tea outside to sit in the shade cast by the tree. In the autumn the leaves change color, and when the winds begin to blow, the leaves flutter to the ground, leaving the branches bare once again.

Why should you care about trees? Why should we make it a priority to safeguard our forests, plant more trees and protect the many diverse plant species we call trees? In *Deep Roots*, we'll have a look at why trees just might be our best friends, *barometers* of how we are looking after our planet, and our partners as we move forward to create a healthier world.

There is nothing more delicious than fresh fruit picked from the tree. Cherries are my all-time favorite treat! BRETT JORGENSEN | DREAMSTIME.COM

I ♥ Trees

Our farm is small—less than a hectare (2 acres)—but since we moved here we have planted dozens of trees. Some (cherry, apple and pear trees) produce fruit each summer. Fast-growing Leyland cypress trees provide shade and act as both a windbreak and privacy screen. Other trees, like the Japanese maples and the blue spruce, we planted because we find them beautiful. Lots of birds, squirrels, insects, bats and other creatures appreciate our decision to plant trees. The tree branches are alive with activity at all times of the year as they provide food, protection and nesting places for many living things.

We use apples picked from trees in our orchard to make pies, applesauce, juice, jelly and fruit leather.
NADEZDA KOROBKOVA | DREAMSTIME.COM

CHAPTER ONE

Earth

Settlers in the western United States and Canada chopped down massive trees like these without considering how long it would take the ancient forests to recover.
LEONARD FRANK, VANCOUVER PUBLIC LIBRARY 5628

FORESTS AND ECOSYSTEMS

Trees have adapted to all kinds of *ecosystems*. Where light, water and nutrients are readily available, trees can grow to incredible sizes. The tallest tree in the world is believed to be a coast redwood tree (*Sequoia sempervirens*) in Redwood National Park in California. At 115.72 meters (379.65 feet) tall, the tree known as Hyperion is about as tall as a forty-story building. The record for the tallest tree keeps changing. Trees grow each year and eventually fall, and a new tallest tree takes its place in the record books.

Where conditions are harsh, trees develop adaptations that help them survive. In most cases, trees like company and live in forests with many other kinds of plants, animals and insects. The particular type of forest changes depending on geography and climate.

The various layers of a forest support different types of plants. Ferns and mosses grow well in the deep shade of the forest floor.
RONNIE COMEAU/STOCKSY.COM

This grove of trembling aspens in Utah is actually a single tree with a massive root system and many stems. Known as Pando, this collection of trunks is believed to be the largest tree on the planet, covering more than 43 hectares (100 acres).
J ZAPELL/WIKIMEDIA.ORG

TREES FEED THE SOIL

A living tree is a big, solid object with a long lifespan. There are many trees all over the world that are estimated to be at least a thousand years old. Eventually, though, even the longest-lived trees die. Disease, insect infestation, windstorms, old age and lightning strikes are just some of the reasons why trees die, but even after a tree has fallen, it is still part of the ecosystem where it spent its life. In a forest, fallen trees soon become a source of nutrition for an army of *detritivores* and *decomposers*, the organisms responsible for the huge job of recycling trees. Tiny beetles, flies and fly larvae, earthworms and various kinds of bacteria and fungi all form part of the army of creatures who break a tree down. Eventually, the tree is no longer recognizable and becomes a part of the dirt of the forest floor.

Sometimes, young trees don't wait until the process of decomposition is complete before starting to grow. In the part

This nurse log provides the perfect place for young seedlings to start growing.
WING-CHI POON/WIKIMEDIA.ORG

of British Columbia where I live, there are many examples of *nurse logs*—old trees that have fallen in the forest. It can take many years for a big tree to be completely broken down into *compost*, but while the process is going on, seeds from plants and trees fall on the rotting log. There is often enough soft material for small roots to take hold, and little trees can start to grow right out of the old stump or log.

The roots of this big old tree cling to the bank of a river. Sometimes tree roots extend a long way beyond the base of the tree, helping to anchor the tree even during windstorms. JAANA LUNNY

HANG ON! USEFUL ROOTS

Growing roots push into the soil and anchor trees so they don't fall over. Those spreading roots help loosen soil and allow water to penetrate the ground, where it can be stored for use during drier weather. They help stop soil from washing away in heavy rains or during floods. When forests are cleared to harvest timber for building, heavy rain hits exposed soil that's no longer protected by the cover of branches and leaves. Dead trees don't soak up water in the same way living trees do, and when the roots themselves die or are removed, rainfall is able to wash away precious topsoil. Not only does this make it harder for new plants to get established, but all that silt and sediment is carried downhill and flushes into streams, rivers and lakes. This silt can cause terrible problems for fish, who are unable to see prey when hunting in the murky water. Their ability to breathe and mate can also be affected.

    Phytoremediation (**fy**-to-ruh-mee-dee-**ay**-shun) is the process of cleaning up soil or water runoff by using plants to remove (and sometimes break down) pollutants. Trees can be really good at phytoremediation, helping to keep the environment healthy. Even though you can't see them, tree roots play a critical role in keeping forest ecosystems in good shape. This is one reason why it's so important to replant trees after an area has been logged.

Try This!

HJALMEIDA/ISTOCK.COM

- Try comparing leaves, needles, flowers or bark from several different types of trees.

- Notice both the similarities and differences between different species.

- Keep a notebook with your observations, diagrams and questions for future investigations.

- Next time you are in a forest, turn over a small patch of dirt with a spade. Using a magnifying glass, investigate how many living things you can find in a shovelful of soil.

11

Dead trees may feed the soil, but living trees draw nutrients up out of the ground so the tree can put them to good use. The right nutrients help trees grow tall and produce fruit, nuts, flowers, nectar and new leaves.

FOREST OR FARM?

Trees don't always die naturally and fall in place. Humans harvest them, sometimes cutting down an entire forest. Often, trees will then be replanted. Depending on the species of trees and the location of the new plantings, trees may be ready to harvest from these plantations in forty to fifty years. A fifty-year-old collection of planted trees isn't quite like a natural forest. A mature forest that has developed on its own is made up of trees of many varieties, ages and sizes. A carefully planted and managed woodlot is made up of tree species selected for particular qualities like speed of growth or the type of wood produced. These man-made forests usually include only one or two types of trees, and those trees are planted over a relatively short period of time.

Intensively planted forests can help prevent additional destruction of *old-growth forests* by providing a source of wood products. All trees, whether growing in a closely controlled environment or in a natural forest, offer many of the same benefits: acting as a *carbon sink* (see page 20), moderating temperature and moisture, and limiting soil *erosion*.

Studying tree rings inside the trunk can tell scientists a lot about climate changes over time. The thickness of each ring will change based on how dry or wet or warm or cool a particular year was. Rings are generally wider during warm years with plenty of moisture.

FOREST FACT: A tree planter in the Canadian bush can plant 1,600 to 5,000 new tree seedlings every day.

Plantations like this one are more like farms than forests and are designed and cared for to maximize production rather than recreate a natural forest ecosystem.

SUGAR0607/DREAMSTIME.COM

One of the most famous parks in the world is Central Park in New York City. Nature lovers Edward Barnard and Ken Chaya created a detailed map of the 341-hectare (843-acre) park, which includes more than 19,000 of the park's 25,000 trees.
KCPHOTOS/ DREAMSTIME.COM

GREENING CITYSCAPES

The term *concrete jungle* refers to a city environment that's densely populated and characterized by a lot of concrete parking lots, roads, bridges and buildings. City planners all over the world have long recognized that trees can make a city more beautiful and less sterile. Even the very largest cities include parks and green spaces to give people a break from man-made structures.

FROM TINY ACORN TO MIGHTY OAK

Considering just how big trees can grow, it's amazing that many of them begin with a seed.

Giant sequoias are among the world's largest trees, but their cones are small—only 4 to 7 centimeters (1.6 to 2.8 inches) long. The cone itself is not a seed, but rather a home for more than 200 tiny seeds, each only about the width of a grain of salt! These trees measure their lifespans in hundreds of years, so it shouldn't be a surprise that the cones can be very patient. While a few seeds are released each year in hot weather, many wait until a fire passes through the forest. The heat from the fire triggers the cones to open, and out spill many seeds at one time. It can take thirty years before the cones open under exactly the right conditions. All that time, the seeds wait patiently for their chance to land on a patch of fertile soil, where they will begin to grow.

FOREST FACT: Some studies suggest that people who can see trees from their hospital windows heal faster.

It doesn't matter how long your arms are, there's no way you (or even you and a few friends) would be able to hug a mature California redwood tree! The biggest can be nearly 31 meters (100 feet) in circumference.
JCAMILOBERNAL/DREAMSTIME.COM

Wood Works

Some enterprising furniture makers and cabinet builders use old wood from barns and other demolished structures to craft everything from kitchen counters to coffee tables, like this one made from an old wooden door.
QUASARPHOTO/DREAMSTIME.COM

DANI TATE-STRATTON

Skog is a Canadian company that makes fancy engraved wooden items like postcards, writing journals and business cards. Every time a customer makes a purchase, the company makes a donation to The Nature Conservancy's Plant a Billion Trees campaign. Initiatives like this help ensure forests will remain healthy for generations to come.

I ♥ Trees

Planting a tree is a wonderful way to commemorate an important life event—like the birth of a child. When my mother was a baby, her family planted a lilac tree outside her grandmother's house in Germany. For her whole life, my mom loved lilac trees, and to this day I associate the smell of lilac blossoms in spring with warm memories of my mother.

Many family photos were taken in front of the lilac tree outside my great-grandmother's house in Germany.
COURTESY OF NIKKI TATE

Sections of ancient corduroy roads dating back 4,000 years have been found in Glastonbury in England, and there is evidence they were also used by the Romans.
3355M/DREAMSTIME.COM

Mushrooms sticking up from the forest floor are evidence of the hidden mycelium highway below. Though many mushrooms are delicious, some can be deadly. Don't pick and eat any mushrooms unless a knowledgeable adult is there to identify them!
WALDRU/DREAMSTIME.COM

CORDUROY ROADS

Building a road might not be the first thing you think of when you consider how you might use tree trunks. Corduroy roads are built by placing logs side by side across the intended route and then covering the rough base with sand. Though roads like this might make a muddy or swampy area passable, they are not exactly known for being smooth. If the logs are used as a foundation and then covered by something longer-lasting (gravel or even paving), the resulting road can last a surprisingly long time. The Alaska Highway between Burwash Landing and Kaidern in Yukon Territory was built this way and lasted half a century!

MYCELIUM HIGHWAY

A highway of a very different kind lies just out of sight beneath the forest floor. The *mycelium* highway is a complex network of tiny interconnected fibers made up of individual threadlike filaments. The "fruit" of this massive net pops up out of the ground, where we see it and identify it as a mushroom. What travels on the highway? Bacteria migrate along the pathways and, as they go, perform functions as varied as breaking down toxic chemicals into harmless molecular components or extracting minerals from rock. Those minerals then travel to the finest hairs of plant roots, where they are absorbed. Nutrients carried along the fine tendrils of the mycelial mat help feed the massive trees living in the forest above. In some cases, the network carries diseases that can have a negative impact on the trees or other plants.

Scientists are only now beginning to understand the important role this underground transportation network plays in forest ecology, but as studies continue, mycelium may be used in oil-spill cleanups, water-filtration systems or even as a possible replacement for Styrofoam!

It's said that the spiritual teacher known as Gautama Buddha sat beneath a tree like this and attained enlightenment. To honor this event, many Buddhist temples around the world (like this one in Thailand) plant ficus trees. WIKIPEDIA.ORG/DIEGO DELSO

I ♥ Trees

I love picking fresh peas, beans, cucumbers and tomatoes from my garden. Vegetables are happiest when they live in healthy soil and get plenty of sunshine, water and good nutrition. Some of my most productive garden beds are those I built using the hügelkultur system, which mimics the way soil is built in the forest. The bottom layer of the garden bed is made of logs, which slowly decompose over time. As they rot, they release nutrients and provide food for worms, insects and microorganisms. I pile smaller sticks, twigs and leaves over the thicker logs, and compost, leaves and soil on top of that.

The first layer in a hügelkultur bed is often full of logs like this one.
DANI TATE-STRATTON

CHAPTER TWO

Air

GREEN LUNGS

Trees may look as if they are just standing around, but in fact they are very busy. Through their leaves or needles they breathe in *carbon dioxide* (CO_2) and breathe out oxygen as part of the process of *photosynthesis* (making food energy from sunlight), a very handy trick given that humans and other animals breathe in oxygen and breathe out carbon dioxide. Carbon dioxide is also one of the components of car exhaust, so trees are also busy cleaning CO_2 out of the air at a rate of just over 6,000 kilograms (6.6 tons) every year for each hectare (2.4 acres) of trees.

One hectare of trees pumps out enough oxygen to keep forty people alive and breathing!
SUGIYONO83/DREAMSTIME.COM

There is perhaps no better way to enjoy a tree than to scramble up into its branches with a friend. ISABEL POULIN/DREAMSTIME.COM

This walkway in Penang Island National Park in Malaysia is built 15 meters (50 feet) above the ground, which gives visitors a chance to take a good look at the forest canopy. HAFIZISMAIL/DREAMSTIME.COM

Deforestation contributes to erosion. Responsible foresters plant new trees as soon as possible after cutting, which helps hold soil in place during rainy periods and flooding.
EPPIC/DREAMSTIME.COM

WHAT'S A CARBON SINK?

Anything that is able to absorb CO_2 and keep it out of the atmosphere is called a *carbon sink*. Trees and forests are excellent carbon sinks, sucking up and storing huge amounts of CO_2. This CO_2 is released when the forests burn or when trees fall and slowly rot. Planting trees is a good way to help reduce the effects of excessive CO_2 production. Unfortunately, rapid *deforestation* (for fuel and building materials, and to clear land for agriculture and housing) is making it difficult to plant enough trees to replace those that have been cut down.

FOREST FACT: Each species of fig tree (there are many) requires a specific species of wasp for pollination.

LOOK WAAAAY UP

One of the world's richest ecosystems is one very few of us will ever get to see because it's located way, way up in the rainforest canopy. Sometimes the lowest limbs of rainforest trees start high above the forest floor, which makes access to the complex community living up in the treetops very difficult.

In the redwood forests of California, scientists discovered berry bushes growing in the very tops of the giant trees, where enough dust and dirt can accumulate in hollows and forks to support the growth of other plants. In tropical rainforests, many creatures spend their entire lives high above the ground. Scientists estimate that 100 million different species of *arthropods* live in forest canopies. Those insects and spiders provide food for birds, frogs, lizards, small mammals and other creatures that also live high in the trees.

Wood Works

KOKOPOPSDAVE/ISTOCK.COM

Rather than burning used shipping pallets (which adds to greenhouse gases and contributes to climate change), more and more people consider pallet wood to be a cheap type of building material.

I ♥ Trees

For as long as I can remember I have loved climbing trees. Even though I am usually afraid of heights, for some reason I always feel quite safe when I'm sitting up in the branches of a tree. My old apple trees are a lot of fun to climb, especially early in the fall when their branches are full of apples. I never get tired of climbing up into the branches, reaching out for an apple and taking a bite. Yum!

This tree in Australia begged to be climbed! I was only about three years old and the tree didn't have many branches, but that didn't stop me from trying!
HELGA WILLIAMS

This plant is an example of an epiphyte.
TANOR/ISTOCK.COM

KOALAS LOVE THEIR LEAVES

Some animals spend much of their lives without ever touching the ground. Koalas don't consume a lot of food, partly because they sleep eighteen to twenty hours each day.

Even though eucalyptus leaves contain toxins and don't have a lot of nutritional value, koalas are so well adapted to life in the trees and their strange diet, they are able to extract enough water from the unpalatable leaves that they rarely need to drink.

EPIPHYTES—PLANTS IN THE AIR

Epiphytes are plants that grow on other plants without causing their hosts any harm. Trees support many types of epiphytes, like moss, ferns and orchids. Though these plants might be located far above the ground, they take water and nutrients from the air and fog swirling through the forest canopy.

I ♥ Trees

I love to garden and am very fortunate to live in a place with enough room to plant trees. One of my favorite trees is a eucalyptus, planted when it was just a tiny twig. Now towering up over the pond, the tree reminds me of the early part of my childhood when I lived in Australia.

Something I try to keep in mind when I'm deciding where to plant a tree is how big it will eventually grow!
DANI TATE-STRATTON

Koalas survive mostly by eating eucalyptus leaves.
MAX EAREY /DREAMSTIME.COM

BAZILLMER/ISTOCK.COM

Design the tree house of your dreams. Think about what type of tree would best support your structure. Consider what recycled building materials you could use. Draw a floorplan as well as diagrams showing what the tree house will look like from each side. If you are lucky enough to have a tree in your backyard, maybe you can get an adult to help you build your dream house.

These fast-growing poplar trees are a popular choice for windbreaks. DANI TATE-STRATTON

TREE HOUSES

Building a tree house is one way those of us who are not canopy scientists can get a feel for what life is like far above the ground. Often, tree houses are built using materials taken from the surrounding forest, though people have built tree houses using recycled supplies like shipping pallets or wood scavenged from old building sites. Some ancient trees are hollow inside, and enterprising builders have used the natural infrastructure to create homes and shelters.

TREES WITH ROOTS IN THE AIR

Of the world's eight species of baobabs, six can be found on the island of Madagascar (located off the southeast coast of the African continent). Baobabs don't really have their roots in the air, but they certainly look a bit upside down with their smooth trunks and cluster of branches right at the top. These trees have adapted to life in a very dry climate by storing water in their massive trunks during the rainy season, which is also the only time of year when the baobabs have leaves. When everything else in the area shrivels up in the heat of the dry season, the baobabs produce fruit. This nutritious food sustains animals and insects when there is little else around to eat, which is why the baobab is also known as the Tree of Life.

STOP THAT WIND!

Wind howling across open fields can blow away the topsoil needed for raising healthy crops. One way to stop this loss is to plant windbreaks. Rows of trees (or a combination of trees, shrubs and bushes) not only slow the wind, but also provide shelter and habitat for wildlife and pollinating insects.

Baobab flowers bloom at night and are pollinated by bats.

Even though palms are more closely related to grasses than trees (they have fibrous stems rather than woody trunks), they still provide shade on a hot day.

FOG DRINKERS

It may seem impossible for trees to survive in places where it doesn't rain a lot. Fog, made of water droplets suspended in the air, contains a surprising amount of moisture. Some forests take advantage of this water source by using leaves to drink in moisture and the nutrients the fog contains. In the redwood forests of California, it's estimated that trees might take in as much as half the water they need from the fog during the summer when very little rain falls in the area.

GO PLAY IN THE WOODS

Having trouble concentrating? Studies suggest that spending some time outside in nature helps students concentrate better once back inside the classroom. Students who spent the same amount of time outside but not in contact with plants and trees did not experience the same benefits. Something about the way we interact with trees is good for us in ways we don't fully understand.

Try This!

HONORED/DREAMSTIME.COM

Spending time in the forest is a great way to see wildlife. Patience, a good camera, a tripod and clothing that blends in with the environment will help you capture a great shot! Some wildlife photographers also build special hiding places (called blinds) using sticks, twigs, branches and leaves to better hide from their shy subjects.

Wood Works

NIKKI TATE

When we renovated our kitchen, we found someone online who was demolishing a house. We picked up the old oak cabinets and transformed them with stain and new door handles, creating a lovely kitchen without having to purchase any wood. The project was good for us and kind to the environment.

FOREST FACT: A *chemotherapy* drug used in cancer treatments is extracted from yew trees.

CHAPTER THREE

Water

Not all forests are on land. Kelp forests don't actually include any trees, but the gigantic algae (which can grow to 45 meters, or 150 feet, or longer) provide a source of nourishment and shelter for fish and animals and live by photosynthesis, just like their land-based cousins.
SPIDERMENT/DREAMSTIME

TREES AND THE GLOBAL WATER CYCLE

Imagine a huge underground sponge soaking up millions of gallons of rainwater. That's exactly what tree roots do after it rains. A tree needs to drink a certain amount of water to stay alive, but the volume of water that is sucked up out of the ground is much greater than what the tree needs to survive. What happens to all the extra water? It is released into the atmosphere, raising the *humidity* of the air. When enough water has been "breathed out" by the trees, it condenses into clouds and then falls as rain.

HOW DO TREES DRINK?

Imagine sipping water through a straw more than 100 meters (350 feet) long! Instead of using one fat straw, trees contain many, many tiny dead cells called *xylem*. Xylem cells are stacked up in long rows, and because they are hollow, the water can move through them just like it does through a straw.

Mangrove trees like these on Zanzibar Island are specially adapted to survive in salty water. NICO SMIT/DREAMSTIME.COM

So what makes the water move up instead of down? Water molecules like to stick together. As each water molecule *evaporates* from tiny holes in tree leaves (called *stomates* or *stomata*), it drags along the next water molecule in line behind it. Amazingly, this pull is so powerful inside the tiny tubes of xylem, water from the ground can be dragged high into the forest canopy.

TREES CREATE RAIN

The world's oceans are salty, but the water that evaporates from their surface is fresh. Just like water that evaporates or is breathed out from a forest, fresh water condenses and rains back down on the land. Water that started out in the oceans, though, tends to fall within a narrow strip of land along the shore. Beyond about 240 kilometers (150 miles) from shore, trees are responsible for much of the rain that falls. Moisture sucked up through the roots and expelled through pores in tree leaves condenses and eventually falls as rain in areas even many hundreds of kilometers inland. In places like Australia, where many trees have been cut down, deserts are growing bigger.

FOREST FACT: Not all wood floats. Very heavy, hard woods are known as ironwood. They are so dense they sink in water!

Satellite photo of the Great Green Wall.
NASA/WIKIPEDIA.COM

THE GREAT GREEN WALL

So how do you stop a desert from spreading? One solution is being tried in sub-Saharan Africa, where a tree-planting project known as the Great Green Wall of the Sahara and the Sahel is hoping to slow or reverse the spread of the Sahara Desert. If all goes according to plan, trees will be planted in an area 7,000 kilometers (4,350 miles) long and 15 kilometers (9.3 miles) wide.

WELCOME TO THE OASIS

An *oasis* is a welcome resting place in the middle of a desert. When an underground source of water bubbles up to the surface, various plants soon take hold and begin to grow. Trees thriving at the water's edge are often visible from miles away. In places like Syria, trade routes followed tracks across the desert and led from one oasis to another. Traders in search of a place to stay or somewhere to rest and water their animals found everything they needed at each oasis. Those who controlled the oases controlled the trade routes.

For anyone on a trek across a desert, an oasis is a sight for sore eyes. One of the most beautiful oases in the world is Huacachina, known as the Oasis of America and located in southwestern Peru. About 100 people call Huacachina home.
INGO MEHLING/WIKIPEDIA.COM

I ♥ Trees

When I was a child, I loved it when my grandmother came to visit us from her home in Germany—she was a great storyteller and always had lots of interesting ideas about how the world worked. On one visit she said, "If you cut down all the trees, you will create a desert." I laughed, thinking that it worked the other way—obviously trees could not grow well in a desert without rain. In fact, my grandmother was right. Most of the rain that falls inland is because of trees "breathing out" water.

My grandmother nurtured a wide variety of plants and trees in her garden in Germany.
HELGA WILLIAMS

Wood Works

Our kayaks are made of plywood, a type of board made of thin layers of wood glued together. A layer of fiberglass adds strength and makes these kayaks tough and waterproof.

AH, COOL!

If you've ever taken shelter under a tree on a hot summer day, you will know how effectively a tree can lower the temperature on the ground even when the sun is blazing. At the same time that the tree is blocking the sun's rays from reaching the ground, it is also breathing out a mixture of water and oxygen through the stomates in its leaves. This evaporating water takes heat with it, also cooling the air. A forest can store large amounts of heat, which is released when surrounding temperatures drop. Forests help stop wind from howling across open areas, which also helps keep the temperature from dropping quite as low as in unprotected areas during the winter.

DRINK UP!

As tree roots drink in water, they also absorb nutrients like nitrogen, phosphorous or potassium carried by the water. The sheer volume of water some trees can take in is astonishing. A mature pecan tree can use more than 750 liters (200 gallons) of water on a very hot day during the growing season. The water doesn't stay inside the tree (or the tree would balloon up and burst!) but travels up from the roots, through the trunk, branches, twigs and leaves, where the excess is released into the atmosphere as water vapor and oxygen.

A FEAST OF FISH

Each autumn millions of salmon swim from the Pacific Ocean and head for the west coast of North America in search of a river mouth. Salmon don't swim upstream on just any river—they return to the same place where they were born. It makes sense that predators like eagles and bears eagerly await the return of the salmon each year, but the fish are just as important as a

The leftovers from this bear's meal of salmon will make a nutritious snack for a tree. RWHARR/DREAMSTIME.COM

source of nutrition for the forests of the region. No, trees of the Pacific Northwest don't have teeth, but when fish are dragged out of the river and partially eaten by other animals, the remains are left lying around on the ground. After they decay, nutrients are absorbed into the soil of the forest floor. There, roots from the great trees draw the nutrients upward, nourishing the trees. This is one of the reasons why the trees of the coastal regions of the Pacific Northwest get so big.

Streams where salmon spawn (lay their eggs) need trees to stay healthy. If trees are removed from alongside salmon-bearing rivers, too much silt and dirt washes into the water and prevents the fish from being able to successfully hatch their eggs, which need clear water and unclogged gravel beds to survive.

I ♥ Trees

The Wind in the Willows *by Kenneth Grahame is one of my favorite books. Every time I see a weeping willow's trailing branches, I think of Ratty and Mole paddling their boat along the river, water-loving willow trees always nearby. I think of those characters nearly every morning when I walk down to the field where I keep my sheep. A huge weeping willow not only provides shade for new lambs but is also good protection from hungry eagles who might want to snatch one of the newborns.*

Weeping willows provide shade for this new lamb.
NIKKI TATE

FOREST FACT: Old wooden sailing ships have knees! The bent pieces of wood that support the deck are known as knees. Those made from a single piece of a wood like oak are incredibly strong because the grain of the wood naturally runs along the entire length of what was once a bent branch. A "knee" may also be a piece split from the part of a stump where the root meets the trunk.

Try This!

DREAMSTIME.COM

It's fun to make a wooden boat. Experiment with changing the shape of the boat, how much it's hollowed out, and the type of wood you use to come up with a design that carries a lot of weight, sails well or moves quickly through the water.

Lake Kariba in Zimbabwe is the world's largest man-made lake. Though such a large body of water serves a valuable function as a reservoir, the effect of damming a river can be devastating for existing vegetation and forests. BLUEYEH/DREAMSTIME.COM

WOODEN BOATS

Have you ever built a miniature boat using twigs or scraps of wood and set it adrift? Since people first figured out how to travel over water, trees have been used in shipbuilding. The earliest dugout canoes, made from a single hollowed-out log, date back about 8,000 years. The inside of the boat was sometimes hollowed out by burning sections of the log and then chipping away the charred wood.

In Madagascar, traditional fishing boats are made from wood.

CHAPTER FOUR

Fire

Sticks, twigs, sawdust and bark can all be useful as fuel for cooking fires.
GLENBOW ARCHIVES/NA-1234-5

WOOD AS FUEL

Nobody is quite sure when people started using fire to keep warm and cook food, but the regular, controlled use of fire meant a lot of changes in how people lived. By cooking some foods, more nutrients are made available during digestion. Some believe this might have made it easier for people to get the nutrition they needed to stay healthy. Light from a fire also meant that certain activities could take place after nightfall, and, of course, fire provides heat so people were more comfortable and burned less food energy to stay warm. Fire also offered some protection against animals and biting insects.

Each year many forest fires are started by lightning strikes. LIVINGCANVAS/ISTOCK.COM

NEW LIFE AFTER FIRE

Forest fires are sometimes started by careless campers who don't put out their campfires, but they are also started naturally by lightning strikes. Though forest fires are terrifying, especially when they come close to places where people have built their homes, these blazes are a normal part of the life cycle of some types of forest. Some trees, like *conifers* (evergreen trees with cones and needles instead of leaves) love to grow in areas where fires occasionally burn, and some species (as we found out in Chapter One) actually need to have their cones heated up in a fire before the cones will open and release their seeds.

Douglas fir trees appreciate a fire every now and then. As long as the blaze isn't too hot, the thick, craggy bark of these trees resists burning and protects the tree. When other species fall, the Douglas firs are able to take advantage of the extra sunlight that comes into areas that were heavily treed previously.

Knowing some basic campfire safety tips could save a whole forest from burning.

1. Clear away any dry grass and branches, and dig a hollow.

2. Put rocks around the edge of your fire pit.

3. Keep a bucket of water and a spade close by while your fire is burning.

4. Don't let your fire get too big, and never leave it unattended.

5. Make sure the fire is out completely. Pour water over the embers, stir and cover with sand or dirt. Stir and keep adding water until the ashes are cold.

Sometimes, controlled forest fires like this one in Central Florida are used to prevent more serious wildfires that can burn out of control and destroy thousands of hectares of trees, threaten buildings and take lives.

TFAWLS /DREAMSTIME

The surviving trees grow taller and their seedlings are able to sprout in the more open areas. Because Douglas firs grow a bit more quickly than some of the other tree species in their area, they do well in the years following a fire.

ASH ENHANCES SOIL

Ash left behind after a wood fire can provide nutrients to the soil. Gardeners who love tomatoes, for example, might place a bit of wood ash in each hole before planting their young tomato plants out in the garden. Ash can also be used to discourage slugs and snails. These unwanted visitors to the garden don't like to slide across ash sprinkled on top of the soil around precious plants, though the ash barrier only works when it's dry. If a little ash is a good thing, a lot isn't necessarily better. Adding too much ash will change the *pH* (acidity) level of the soil, which can affect how certain plants will grow.

DIRTY ASH, CLEAN SOAP

Back before people went to the store to buy soap, they made it themselves. One of the ingredients used in the soap-making process is lye, which can be extracted from wood ash by soaking ashes in water. When lye is combined with animal fat and then boiled, soap is the end product!

LET'S DANCE!

Fires are at the center of all kinds of celebrations. Many northern European countries celebrate the *summer solstice* (the longest day of the year) with large bonfires. In Denmark, bonfires were traditionally believed to frighten away evil spirits. Halloween is another festival when it's common to gather around a bonfire. Dressing up in costumes is part of the fun!

Wood Works

STOCKSOLUTIONS/ISTOCK.COM

Sawdust is a waste product left over after trees have been milled (cut into useful pieces of lumber). Sawdust can be compressed and then formed into pellets that are all the same shape and size. These uniform pellets burn slowly and evenly and are a great way to use up material that would otherwise be wasted.

In Bulgaria, participants dance around a bonfire to celebrate.
HUCKGOBLIN/DREAMSTIME.COM

WARMING UP WINTER

The Romans brought evergreen branches inside during the winter celebration of Saturnalia. Burning a yule log has been part of midwinter celebrations in many European countries for centuries.

GREAT BALL OF FIRE

Autotrophs are organisms that produce their own food using energy from sunlight. The sun, a massive ball of fire created by chemical reactions, drives this process, and plants have found many ways to adapt so they can make their own food most efficiently. Leaves and needles are typically thin, in order to expose the greatest surface area possible to the sun. Inside the leaf cells, *chlorophyll* breaks apart water molecules, releasing oxygen into the atmosphere (a good thing because that's what we breathe) and then combining the remaining hydrogen atoms with various other simple elements (like carbon taken from carbon dioxide in the atmosphere and nitrogen drawn up from

I ♥ Trees

When we first came to Canada, our family went camping, which was my first experience with building a bonfire. The campgrounds we visited provided huge piles of wood to campers for free. It was only after we moved to Canada that I learned to enjoy camping food like baked beans, roasted marshmallows and hot dogs.

Food cooked over an open fire always seems to taste better!
INTST/DREAMSTIME.COM

the soil) to form sugars, fats and proteins. Without plants and trees constantly doing this work, we wouldn't have much to eat! Either we eat plant matter directly or we consume products like meat, eggs or milk that come from animals that ate plants.

SLASH-AND-BURN AGRICULTURE

As demand for farmland increases, it's tempting to clear large areas of forest to make room for crops. Land may be cleared to provide food for local residents or it may be used to grow cash crops like soy, coffee or cocoa, or to raise cattle for beef that can be sold to markets elsewhere. Large areas of forested land can be cleared quickly by controlled burning. The ash left behind enriches the soil in the short term, but nutrients are used quickly, which means food production decreases unless farmers find ways to replace the ash-fertilized soil.

FOREST FACT: A *dendro-climatologist* is a scientist who studies tree growth patterns to learn about climate change over time.

Burning down a forest to create new fields for agriculture is not considered to be a sustainable way of managing farmland.
THAI NOIPHO/DREAMSTIME.COM

CONCLUSION

Whether they are used as a source of medicine to heal the sick, firewood to warm us during cold winter nights, or shade to protect us from the broiling sun, trees have enjoyed profound and complicated relationships with people for thousands of years.

Not only are they beautiful to look at, but the forests of the world provide us with food and fuel, and they help keep our air clean and the landscape green. And yet, because we see them all the time, we often don't appreciate just how special—and valuable—our tall green friends really are.

Each spring when the cherry blossoms are in bloom, people in Japan enjoy the tradition of hanami (flower viewing).
XIXINXING/ISTOCK.COM

Recreational tree climbing classes are becoming more and more popular. Kids climb safely high above the ground using special equipment. PETER JENKINS, TREE CLIMBERS INTERNATIONAL, INC.

Acknowledgments

This book would not have been possible without the dedicated work of tree lovers the world over. For many years I have been inspired by people who plant, nurture, study and celebrate trees in all their glorious incarnations. The team at Orca has, once again, proven to be talented and professional as this project was taken from seed to maturity. Many thanks to the readers who provided ideas and inspiration as I worked on this addition to the Footprints series. But mostly, I have to thank the trees themselves, who have been companions and guardians, providers of oxygen, shade, comfort and solace during many long walks through the woods, exuberant swings, homes to tree houses and sources of the best apples I've ever climbed a tree to pluck.

Resources

Books

Hugo, Nancy Ross, & Robert Llewellyn. *Seeing Trees: Discover the Extraordinary Secrets of Everyday Trees.* Portland: Timber Press, 2011.

Lieutaghi, Pierre. *Trees: The Balance of Life, the Beauty of Nature.* Toronto: Duncan Baird Publishers, 2011.

Pakenham, Thomas. *Meetings with Remarkable Trees.* New York: Random House, 1998.

Parker, Edward, & Anna Lewinton. *Ancient Trees: Trees that Live for a Thousand Years.* London: Batsford, 2013.

Resources

Books cont'd

Rodd, Tony, & Jennifer Stackhouse. *Trees: A Visual Guide.*
    Oakland: University of California Press, 2008.
Suzuki, David, & Wayne Grady. *Tree: A Life Story.*
    Vancouver: Greystone Books, 2009.

Websites

Benefits of Trees: www.ncsu.edu/project/treesofstrength/
benefits.htm
Cloud Forest: www.canopyintheclouds.com
Forest Ecology Educational Tools: www.sierraclub.bc.ca/
education/
Huacachina Oasis: www.atlasobscura.com/places/
huacachina-oasis
Hügelkultur: www.permaculture.co.uk/articles/
many-benefits-hugelkultur
Redwood National Park: www.nps.gov/redw/index.htm
Sahara Desertification: www.education.nationalgeographic.com/
news/great-green-wall/
Saving Old Growth Forests: www.wildernesscommittee.org/
oldgrowth
SKOG: www.skog.ca
Trees and Climate Change: ltrr.arizona.edu/about treerings
Windbreaks: www.rhs.org.uk/advice/profile?PID=624

Glossary

arthropod—an invertebrate animal, such as an insect or spider, having an external skeleton, a segmented body and jointed appendages

autotroph—an organism that provides its own food using energy from sunlight

barometer—an instrument for determining the pressure of the atmosphere; also, generally, something that measures fluctuations

carbon dioxide (CO_2)—a gas that is produced when people and animals breathe out or when certain fuels are burned, and that is used by plants for energy

carbon sink—anything that is able to absorb CO_2 and keep it out of the atmosphere, such as trees and forests

chemotherapy—a type of cancer treatment that uses drugs to destroy cancer cells

chlorophyll—the green substance in plants that makes it possible for them to make food from carbon dioxide and water

compost—a decayed mixture of organic matter (such as leaves and grass) that is used to improve soil quality

concrete jungle—a city environment that's densely populated and characterized by a lot of concrete parking lots, roads, bridges and buildings

conifers—evergreen trees with cones and needles instead of leaves

decomposer—an organism (such as an earthworm or a fungus) that feeds on dead and decomposing organic matter

deforestation—the act or result of cutting down or burning all the trees in an area

dendroclimatologist—a scientist who studies tree growth patterns to learn about climate change over time

detritivore—an organism (such as an earthworm or a fungus) that feeds on dead and decomposing organic matter

ecosystem—an intricate system in which everything that exists in a particular environment relies on the other parts of that environment in some way

epiphytes—plants that grow on other plants without causing their hosts any harm

erosion—the gradual destruction of something by natural forces (such as water, wind or ice)

evaporation—the process by which water changes from liquid to gas

gyotaku—ancient Japanese art of covering a fresh fish in ink or paint and then pressing it on paper to make a print

hanami (lit. "viewing flowers")—Japanese traditional custom of enjoying the transient beauty of flowers

hügelkultur (German)—the practice of making raised garden beds or mounds filled with rotting wood, which mimics the way soil is built in a forest

humidity—the amount of water vapor in the air

ironwood—very heavy, hard woods that are so dense they sink in water

milled lumber—wood that has been processed into beams and planks

mycelium—a complex network of tiny interconnected fibers made up of individual threadlike filaments, usually underground, whose fruit becomes a fungus or mushroom aboveground

nurse log—an old tree that has fallen in the forest and provides nutrients to new plants

oasis (pl. oases)—an area in a desert where there is water and plants

old-growth forest—a forest that has attained great age without significant disturbance and thereby exhibits unique ecological features such as diversity in plant and animal species

pH—the scale used to measure the acidity of chemicals, from zero (acidic) to fourteen (basic), where pure water is seven (neutral)

photosynthesis—the process by which a green plant turns water and carbon dioxide into food when the plant is exposed to light

phytoremediation—the process of cleaning up soil or water runoff by using plants to remove (and sometimes break down) pollutants

slash-and-burn—a form of agriculture characterized by felling and burning trees to clear land, especially for temporary agriculture

stomate or stoma (pl. stomates or stomata)—small holes in the leaves of plants where water vapor, oxygen and carbon dioxide are exchanged

summer solstice—when the sun reaches its farthest north position in the northern hemisphere (June 21) or farthest south in the southern hemisphere (December 21)

xylem—a type of tissue found in trees that transports water and nutrients from the roots to the leaves

Index

ORCA FOOTPRINTS

Small steps toward big changes.

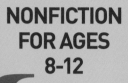
What makes Orca's nonfiction different?

Whether the topic is sustainability, cycling or bees, the Orca Footprints are **PASSION PROJECTS** written by enthusiastic authors who are keen to share their research and experience with young readers.

TOPICS INCLUDE:
- **CYCLING**
- **FOOD PRODUCTION**
- **SUSTAINABLE ENERGY**
- **CLEAN WATER**
- **HOUSING**
- **WASTE AND RECYCLING**
- **BEES**

LOOKING FOR MORE FOOTPRINTS?

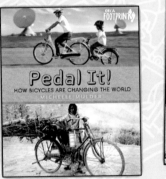

Pedal It!
HOW BICYCLES ARE CHANGING THE WORLD
MICHELLE MULDER

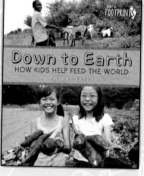

Down to Earth
HOW KIDS HELP FEED THE WORLD
NIKKI TATE

Brilliant!
SHINING A LIGHT ON SUSTAINABLE ENERGY
MICHELLE MULDER

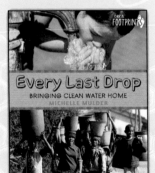

Every Last Drop
BRINGING CLEAN WATER HOME
MICHELLE MULDER

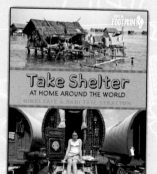

Take Shelter
AT HOME AROUND THE WORLD
NIKKI TATE & DANI TATE-STRATTON

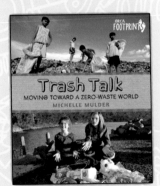

Trash Talk
MOVING TOWARD A ZERO-WASTE WORLD
MICHELLE MULDER

What's the Buzz?
KEEPING BEES IN FLIGHT

www.orcafootprints.com